Sheila McCullagh

Indians in the Painted Desert

Longman

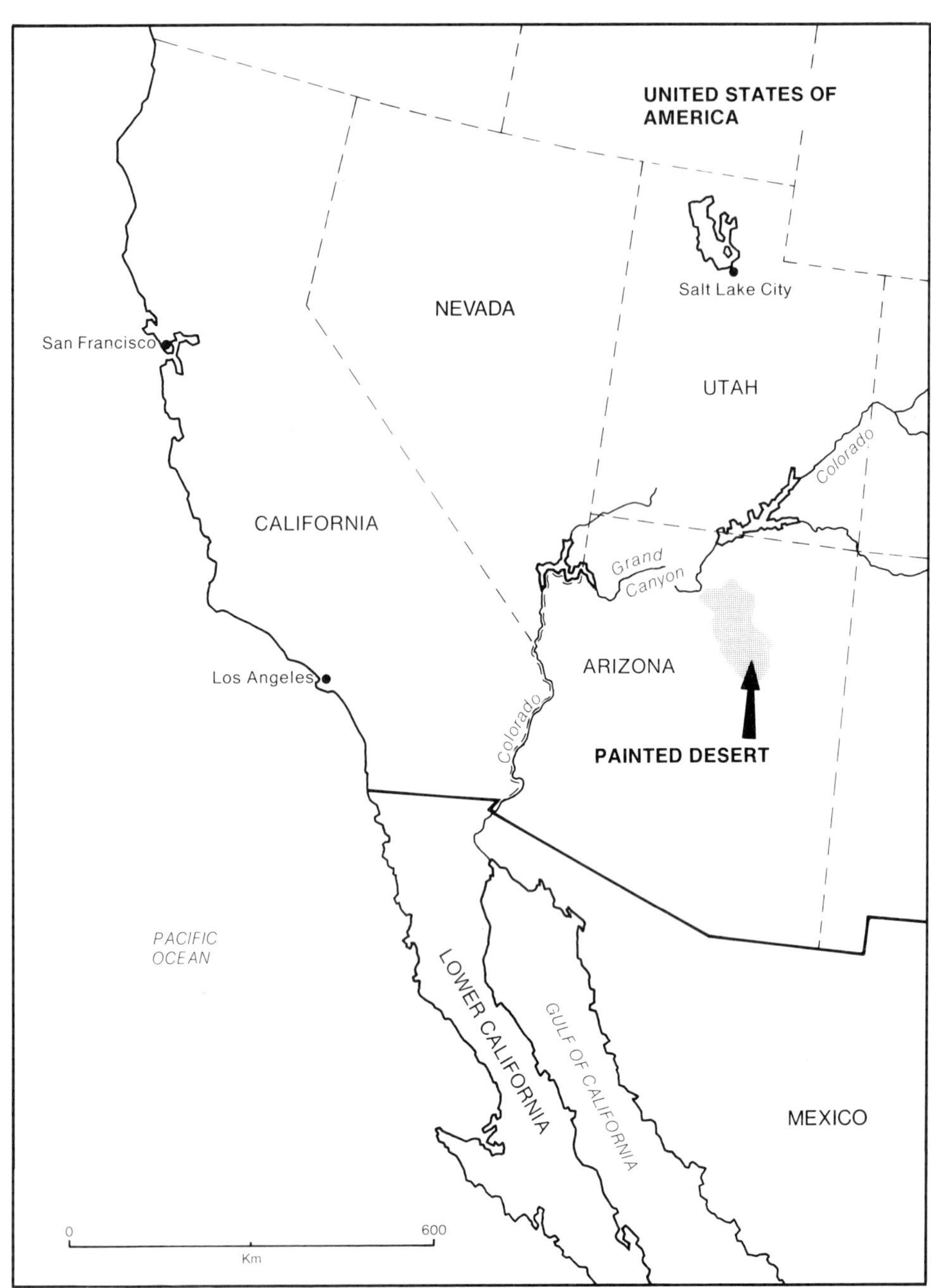
UNITED STATES OF AMERICA
NEVADA
Salt Lake City
UTAH
San Francisco
CALIFORNIA
Colorado
Grand Canyon
ARIZONA
Los Angeles
Colorado
PAINTED DESERT
PACIFIC OCEAN
LOWER CALIFORNIA
GULF OF CALIFORNIA
MEXICO
0
600
Km

Today, North American Indians often live in cities and towns, but there are some places where they live together in clans or tribes, and maintain their own way of life.

One of these places is the Painted Desert. The Painted Desert lies in the American south west, in the State of Arizona. It is well-named: in many places the earth and stones and cliffs are brilliant red, and in others they are white and yellow and brown. There are mounds of blue and grey clays, and all kinds of minerals in the earth. Very little rain falls on the desert: sometimes there is none at all for a whole year. But in a good season, enough rain falls to keep the desert plants alive, and the occasional springs of water flowing. Then blue-green sage-brush and mounds of yellow daisies, called dodgeweed, add to the colours of the ground. The air is very dry and the sky over the desert is a deep blue, with a few small clouds. When rain comes, it often falls in fierce storms of thunder and lightning.

Much of the land belongs to two tribes, the Hopi Indians and the Navaho Indians. This is their country. Although some of them drive cars, go to schools and colleges, and sometimes work together with the Americans who live near their homes, in many ways they still keep to a way of life which is their own. They are a proud people, with their own ideas and beliefs and ways of doing things.

Echo Cliffs in the Painted Desert.
The land is high –
over 1,000 metres above sea level.
The days are hot,
but the nights can be cold.

Some animals manage to live in the desert. Prairie dogs dig out their homes.

Chipmunks can live on seeds even in very dry places.

The Petrified Forest

A log of petrified wood

The Petrified Forest – a forest of fallen trees, which have turned into stone – lies to the south of the Painted Desert.

200 million years ago, this was an area of heavy rainfall, of swamps and streams. Great trees grew here, over 60 metres high. When the trees fell, the logs were carried down by the streams into swamps.

The streams brought down mud and sand. The water was full of tiny crystals of quartz, and of minerals, which soaked into the wood, and remained there, while the trees were buried deep in sand and mud.

The minerals were left as the water soaked away, and slowly the trees changed into stone.

The climate changed and the land became dry. Few plants grew and the wind began to blow the soil away, until the trees were uncovered again.

The Indians of today are the descendants of the first people to live in North America. We sometimes say that America was 'discovered' by Christopher Columbus, in 1492. But men first discovered America about fifty thousand years ago. In those days, there was a bridge of land, hundreds of kilometres wide, from Asia to Alaska, across what is now the Bering Sea. Animals, looking for food, wandered across the land bridge into North America. Human beings followed them, hunting the animals. They didn't all come at once. They probably followed in groups and families over perhaps thousands of years, until the land bridge sank under the sea. These were the people whom we know today as North American Indians. Over thousands of years, they slowly spread out through North and South America. Some of them settled in the northern forests, in Canada. Some of them stayed on the prairies, the great grasslands in the centre of North America, and lived chiefly by hunting. But some of them found their way southwards and eastwards, until they reached the sea.

There are still traces in the Painted Desert, and the surrounding country, of Indians who first lived there about 1,500 to 2,000 years ago.
one knows what they called themselves,
ie Navaho Indians of today gave them the name
'Anasazi', the 'Ancient Ones'.

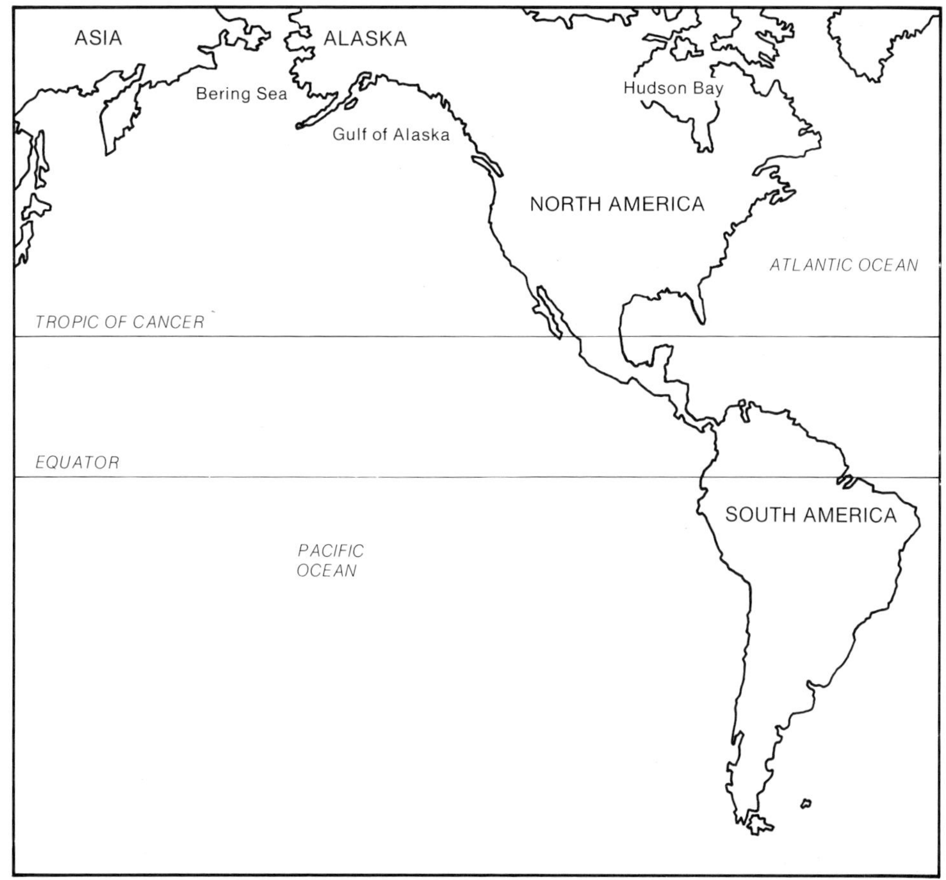

The first Anasazi lived in simple houses. They dug a round pit into the ground, about a metre deep, and lined the walls with logs. They roofed the houses with brushwood, fastened to a centre pole. But about a thousand years ago, the Anasazi began to build houses of stone. They built in open country, but they also built in caves in the walls of the canyons, the steep sided valleys they found in the Painted Desert.

The steep side of the Canyon de Chelly, with the ruins of Anasazi houses in a cave in the cliff wall.

A closer view of the ruins on the opposite page. (The name 'Canyon de Chelly' comes from a Navaho word, meaning 'rock canyon'. It is pronounced 'de Shay'.)

The Anasazi began to build their finest houses about the year 1100. They chose the sites carefully.

In the Canyon de Chelly most of the houses are built at least fifteen metres above the floor of the canyon. Most of them were built in caves on the north side, where they are shaded from the high, hot sun in summer, but where the winter sun, which is lower in the sky, can shine on the houses and help to keep them warm.

corn

The Anasazi hunted animals for food, but they also grew Indian corn. In Europe, 'corn' means wheat and oats and barley, but in America 'corn' means 'corn-on-the-cob', or maize. The Anasazi could eat the cobs when they were fresh, or they could dry them, and keep them for the winter.

Corn will keep for up to two years in the dry desert air, and the Anasazi ground it into flour with stones, as they needed it. They made baskets, in which to store their corn, from the fibres of the Yucca plants, which grow in the desert. These were so cleverly made, that the first Anasazi are called 'The Basket Makers'.

yucca

On the edge of the Painted Desert, the ground sometimes rises to more than two thousand metres. It is high enough to catch the rain clouds which blow in from the south west, and woods of pine trees can grow. Deer live in the woods. The Anasazi hunted deer. They hunted prairie dogs, and the pronghorn antelopes which still wander across the country. But because they planted corn, too, the Anasazi settled down to live in places where there was water.

The people reached their houses by long wooden ladders, or by climbing up from the roofs of lower houses to the doors of higher ones. By building in open caves along the cliffs, the Anasazi saved the space on the floors of canyons for their crops. Their houses were within reach of the winter sun, and they could be defended against enemies.

The Anasazi built their stone cities, and lived in them for two or three hundred years, and then something happened. About the end of the thirteenth century, the stone cities in the Painted Desert and the canyons were deserted. The Anasazi left them and moved away. No one knows exactly why they left, but it is possible to guess the reasons. There was a long drought from 1279–1299 A.D., when there was very little water in the whole area. We can tell this from the remains of trees. If you cut a tree trunk across you will see that it is built up by rings of wood. Every year, a new ring is added to the trunk. In good years, when there is plenty of water, a thicker ring is added. In years of drought, only a thin ring grows around the tree.

By comparing trees which have grown over the centuries, it has been possible to build up a pattern of tree rings, going back hundreds of years. This means that we know in which years there was plenty of rain, and in which years there was a drought. It also means that it is possible to tell how old any buildings are, where wood is used. If you find an old Indian hut in the desert, you can tell from the pattern of rings in which year the tree was cut which was used for the centre roof pole, or for the walls. So we know that the Anasazi probably left their cities because of a drought. It may be, too, that they had enemies: that other Indian tribes began to raid their fields and villages.

Monument Valley, which borders the Painted Desert in the north.

It is easy to see what a drought would mean. Even in ordinary years, the plants grow far apart, so that the roots of each plant can catch any rain which falls on the ground around it. Where the earth is trodden down on a path or a road, killing the plants, it soon turns to sand. Rocks and cliffs are cut into strange shapes by the wind. Short but heavy storms sometimes break over the land, and the light top soil may be carried away by a sudden rush of water.

In a drought, the plants die, and the thin soil becomes wind-blown sand.

Sand-dunes in Monument Valley

Even in good years, the Indians must go many kilometres with their animals to find enough plants for them to live on. They still make brushwood shelters, as their ancestors did, to sleep in when they are too far from home to get back at night.

A brushwood shelter

The Hopi Indians

The Anasazi vanished from the stone houses which they had built in the Painted Desert and the canyons, but they survived. They moved to the south and west, perhaps joining with other groups of Indians. When the Spaniards first came to the south-western part of North America, about 1540 A.D., they found the Indians living in stone houses similar to some of the older buildings of the Anasazi. The Spaniards called them 'Pueblo Indians', 'Village Indians', because they lived in settled villages and grew corn.

They found the Hopi Indians living in the Painted Desert. The Hopis tell in their stories and legends how the different families, or clans of Hopi Indians, wandered throughout America. They came to a place called Oraibi, which lies in the Painted Desert. 'Hopi' means 'peace', and the Hopi Indians were a peaceful people. According to their many legends and stories, the Hopis came from the west, over the sea, but it may be that they are descendants of the Anasazi. The Hopis still continue the beliefs and ceremonies of their ancestors today. They are divided into families, or 'clans' and each clan is named after the spirit of an animal. The most important clans are the Bear Clan, the Parrot Clan, the Eagle Clan and the Badger Clan. Each clan knows special stories and ceremonies which are an important part of the life of the whole Hopi tribe. The Hopis believe in a Great Spirit, the Creator of all animals and forms of life, and all worlds.

They also believe that animals and plants have spirits, which they call 'Kachinas'. The Hopis have many dances and ceremonies, through which they re-tell the story of the creation of the world. Through these dances, they summon the Kachinas to help them with their lives: to bring them success as hunters or craftsmen.

Kachinas are spirits, and cannot be seen, but at the ceremonies men from different clans dress in special clothes, and wear a mask over their heads, to represent the Kachinas. The Hopi believe that when a man does this, and performs the right dances, the Kachina enters into him, and can be persuaded to use his special powers to help the people.

During the two hundred years, which followed Columbus' voyage, the Spaniards conquered many of the Indian peoples in South and Central America. They tried to force the Hopi to become Christians, and to give up their own beliefs. But the Hopi rose in revolt against the Spaniards, and against any Indians who had been converted by them. Other tribes joined the revolt, and although the Spaniards were able to hold some of the land for a time, the Hopis say proudly that they were never conquered. In 1822, the whole of Mexico gained its freedom from Spain. Although today there are Christian churches and missions among the Hopi, many of the Hopis still keep to their own ancient beliefs and ceremonies and dances. Their religion is an essential part of their lives.

The Hopis want their children to understand the dances and ceremonies. There are many Kachinas, and it is important for the children to learn to recognise each of them. So they make wooden dolls, which they dress exactly as the men are dressed for the Kachina dances, and give them to the children.

When the right ceremony is performed, the Hopi believe that the spirit of the corn will enter the man who is dressed as the corn Kachina. Through his power, their corn will grow.

The Corn Kachina

The Wolf Kachina

All creatures and plants have their own spirit, or Kachina. The dancers wear masks in the ceremonies, and so the dolls are also made with masks.

Many of the dances take place at night and are very exciting, and perhaps even a little frightening, but the purpose of the ceremony is to re-tell the legends, and to persuade the Kachinas to use their power for the good of the Hopis.

The Navaho Indians, and the coming of the Americans

During the sixteenth century, another tribe of Indians found their way to the Painted Desert, and the region round about. They called themselves 'Dineh', which in their language simply means 'The People'. The Hopis called them 'Tasauuh', which meant 'the people who pounded their enemies', because the Tasauuh sometimes killed their captives by hitting them on the head with a rock. They were hunters and fighters, and raided the villages of other Indians. They grew corn, too. (According to Hopi legends, they learnt to grow corn from the Hopis.) The Spaniards called them the Navaho, the Indians of the planted fields, and they are called by this name today. (The name is sometimes spelt Navajo. 'J' is pronounced like 'h' in Spanish.)

During the nineteenth century, the Indians in and around the Painted Desert met a new people, the Americans. People from Europe had settled along the east coast of North America for 300 years, and now they were spreading westwards. With the coming of the Americans, many Indians began to fight for their land. Their whole way of life was threatened by the new settlers. Sometimes they were massacred by soldiers, and they in turn fought back and killed the settlers, and raided the new farms and homes that the Americans were trying to set up on land which the Indians thought was theirs.

The Navahos struggled fiercely against the Americans, and in 1864, the Americans sent expeditions of soldiers against them. The Navahos had raided other Indians too, and some of these joined the Americans. It was a terrible time for the Navaho. Their corn and villages were burnt.

The soldiers rounded up the Navaho people. They had to walk to a place called Fort Sumner, four hundred and eighty kilometres from their 'own country'. The Navahos still speak of it as 'The Long Walk'. Only the very old, and very young children, rode in wagons. It was a time of hunger and bitter unhappiness. The Navaho were a proud people and they knew they had been defeated.

They stayed at Fort Sumner for four years. The Americans gave them food, and tried to settle them there, on new land. But the Navahos longed for their 'own country', the red rocks and cliffs and canyons they had left. They longed for their freedom. They found the food strange, and the water bitter. There were eight or nine thousand Navahos, and the Americans found them an increasing burden to support.

When at last in 1868 the Navahos signed a peace treaty with the Americans, one of their leaders said: 'I hope to God you will not ask me to go to any other country, except my own.'

The Canyon de Chelly

The United States Government gave them seed, to plant corn again, and sheep and cattle, and the Navaho returned to Monument Valley, to the Painted Desert, to the Canyon de Chelly and the land round about. It was a very hard life indeed, especially during the early years of their return. But the Navahos survived, and prospered, and today there are ninety thousand of them, and they are the biggest Indian tribe in the United States. They still live in their 'own country' today.

The Navahos made their last stand against the Americans in the Canyon de Chelly in the Painted Desert. It was the centre of the Navaho country: a place where they had always been able to seek refuge.

The Indians had no means of writing, but they left records on rocks, and on the walls of the canyons, in signs and pictures.

This is a picture of the coming of the Spaniards, on the wall of the Canyon de Chelly. The man in brown in the centre is a priest: his robe is marked with a cross. The Indians in North America had no horses, until the Spaniards came. They traded with the Spaniards, and bought horses, and then bred them themselves.

The Navahos have left records of some of the animals in pictures on the rocks, too. Above is a cougar, a mountain lion.

A pronghorn antelope, painted on the rock wall of the Chanyon de Chelly.

The Navaho Indians today

When they returned to their own land, the numbers of Navaho Indians increased. So did their sheep and cattle. But the soil on their land is poor, and there is only a limited number of plants for sheep and other animals to eat. If too many plants are eaten, the soil becomes bare, and blows away in the wind. To the Navahos, their sheep are more than just a source of food and wool. They are a sign of wealth and importance, so it is difficult for them to agree to limit their numbers. Yet, if there are too many, more of the land returns to desert. Over almost half their land, it takes twenty-five acres to support one sheep.

Today, the Navahos earn their living in many different ways. They still plant corn, and herd sheep, and the women weave the wool from the sheep into rugs and blankets, and sell these in the shops. Some of the Navahos make brooches and necklaces of silver, set with turquoise stones, which they sell. They have always been an adaptable people, quick to learn new ways, and they learnt how to work in silver when they were at Fort Sumner.

They take jobs in the area surrounding their land, and they work for the United States Government, in schools and hospitals. Many of the men were in the army in the Second World War. After it was over, they returned to their own homes in their own land.

A hogan

Some of the Navahos live in modern homes, but many of them still live in the old type of Navaho home, called a 'hogan'. A hogan is a six-sided dwelling, with walls made of logs. There is one large room, usually about 8 metres in diameter. It is warmer in winter than the modern type of house, and cooler in summer.

Everyone has their own place inside it. The men sit on the north side of the hogan, and the women on the south. There are special places for everyone's possessions. The fire is in the centre, and pots and pans are stacked around it.

A family often has more than one hogan, and there is so little rain that it is possible to do many things out of doors.

Today, a car or a 'pick-up truck' often stands outside the hogan. If there is enough water to grow corn, there may be a tractor, too, to cultivate the land.

Navaho herdsmen, watering their horses at a pump. They carry lassos, and water bottles, and wear hats with wide brims, to protect them from the sun.

The picture opposite shows a farm in the Canyon de Chelly. There is a field of corn, and sheep are grazing near the green-roofed hogan. There is a brushwood shelter beside it, which can be used as a store, or for cattle.

Water is close to the surface in the canyon, and so trees can grow there, as well as corn. After rain, a stream runs through the canyon, and it is always possible to find water by digging a well a metre or so deep.

A hogan in the Canyon de Chelly

Both men and women play very important parts in Navaho life. The men usually build the houses, look after the horses and cattle, and do much of the work in the fields. The women are in charge of cooking, and the life of the family inside the hogan. But both help each other. The children are expected to help, too, especially in getting wood for the fire, and in going out each day with the sheep. Nowadays, the men often have a job to go to, too. Many Navaho women still weave blankets and rugs, and they do beadwork. They sell these to tourists, so that they have an independent income of their own.

The Navahos trace their descent (their ancestors) through their mother's rather than their father's family. They do not take their father's name, as people in western society do. There are clan names, and everyone has a special, secret name, which he knows, but does not tell. People often have nicknames, too, but it is very bad manners to call someone by his name. Instead, he may be called 'my friend', or 'my son', or perhaps just 'you'. Of course, when a child goes to school, he or she is expected to have a first name and a last name. Then boys and girls will often give the name of their mother's or their father's clan as their second name, and will choose any name they like for their first name. From time to time, they decide to change their names, and a girl who was once called Ann may decide to be called Mary. One Navaho may use several different names.

One of the reasons why many Navahos live in the older type of house, is that religious ceremonies can be performed only in a hogan. For the Navaho, as for the Hopi, their religion is an essential part of their everyday life, and although some of them have become Christians, very many retain the beliefs and customs of their ancestors.

Many Navaho believe in ghosts, and the power of witches, and feel that they need protection against them. If anyone in a family falls ill, they help him by carrying out ceremonies which will put things right with the forces of nature around him, and help him to feel well again. The ceremonies make the Navaho feel safe and cared for, and protected against possible danger. Like the Hopi, the Navaho believe in spirits, who cannot ordinarily be seen. They call these the 'Holy People', and seek their help through chants and dances and ceremonies.

Some of the Navaho are 'singers': they know the ancient chants, and can carry out the ceremonies which will help their people. The making of a 'dry painting', with sand and pollen and materials gathered in the desert, is a part of the ceremony to help the sick. When someone is ill, his family sends for a singer. (Today, he may of course go to hospital as well.) The singer will spend some days gathering the right herbs and sands, and then he will come to the hogan. The chants are sung, and dry paintings are made on the floor.

Sand painting

This dry painting shows one of the sky people, who is one of the Holy People. She is standing on lightning and holds corn and a tobacco bag in her hands. Every colour and every line of the painting has a special meaning for the Navaho. This is the kind of painting which might be made as part of a 'healing-chant' for someone who is ill.

A 'sing' may last for as much as four days, and a number of paintings will be made. No painting is allowed to remain for more than twelve hours. At the end of the ceremony, the man who is sick sits in the middle of the painting, and the sand is stuck on to his body, bit by bit.

The Navaho sing on many occasions in their lives. They have chants which they sing when they wake up in the mornings, and light the fire, and go out with the sheep. They believe that their songs keep them in touch with nature, and with the Holy People, and make sure that all goes well.

There are many colours of sand in the desert, and the paintings are very colourful – red and yellow, white and black and blue, all made on a background of 'ordinary' sand.

This Navaho woman is wearing a beautiful Navaho brooch, made of silver and turquoise.

A Navaho girl in the Canyon de Chelly

Today, many things are changing in the American southwest. Some changes are helpful, but some are very hard for the people to accept.

Oil has been found on the Navaho Reservation, and this brings in money for the Navahos. The Colorado River has been dammed at Glen Canyon, and a big lake has been made there.

The Glen Canyon Dam.

The dam provides electricity, but a big canyon, which was part of the Navaho lands, was flooded to make it. The Navahos continue to grow in numbers, but the amount of land they have is limited, and they do not want to lose a metre of it.

The Colorado River, controlled by the dam, runs just north of the Painted Desert.

Their problem today is to find ways of making a living, which will allow them to stay in their 'own country'. They want to keep their own traditions, and their own way of life.

Today, you can go to the Painted Desert and Monument Valley, to the Canyon de Chelly and the Petrified Forest. It is possible to drive over some of the roads in a car, although on many roads a landrover or a jeep is the best kind of vehicle. It is not surprising that people want to go there, for this is some of the most beautiful country in the world. The Navahos act as guides, and there are some parts of their country where today you may only go with one of them to guide you.

The Pronghorn antelope still roams wild across the country, but although a Navaho may go hunting occasionally, today he uses a gun. He does not depend on hunting for his food. He buys his meat at the local store.

Yet many of the old ways and beliefs still survive. The songs are still sung and the dances and ceremonies are still performed.

There is still rivalry between the Hopis and the Navahos, but during the struggles against the Spaniards, some of the Hopi and Pueblo Indians found refuge with the Navaho in the Canyon de Chelly, and it is said that the Navahos in that canyon 'have a Pueblo look'.

Perhaps through them, the descendants of the Anasazi, the Ancient Ones, have found their way back to the Canyon de Chelly, where the Indians once more live safely, in their 'own country'.

A young boy in the Canyon de Chelly